daniel eatock

ISBN 978-1-894699-53-2

onomatopee 76

Onomatopee 76: Cabinet Project

One + 1
Daniel Eatock

Producer   Freek Lomme

Graphic design   Sebastian
We Have Photoshop

Photography   Carlo Draisci

Text   Marie-Anne McQuay

Special thanks   David Falkner
Stanley Picker Gallery, Kingston University

Printing   Lecturis, Eindhoven

Edition   500

Made possible thanks to   Municipality of Eindhoven and
Mondriaan Foundation

Onomatopee   Bleekstraat 23
NL 5611 VB Eindhoven
The Netherlands

www.onomatopee.net   info@onomatopee.net

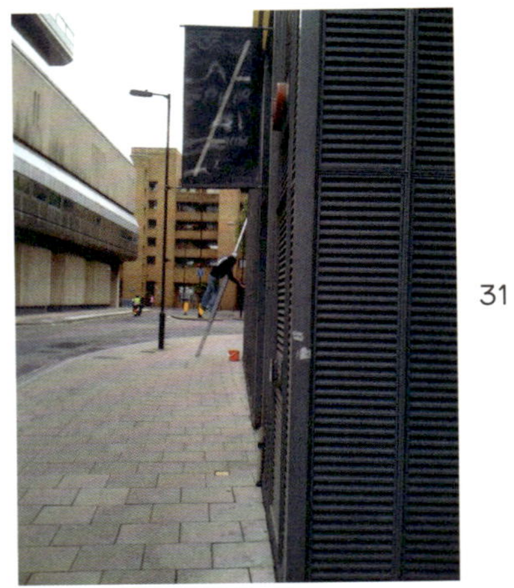

31

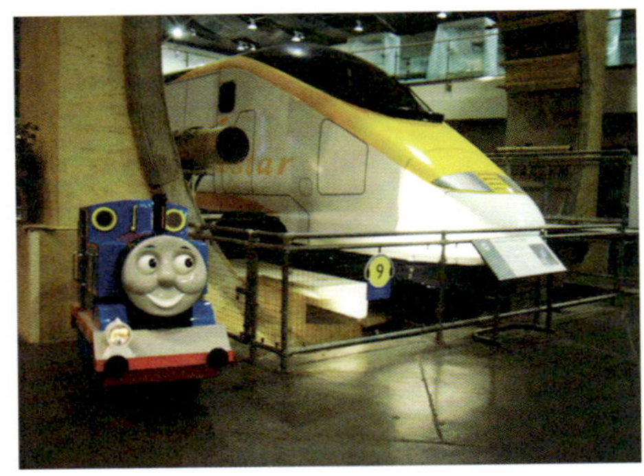

32

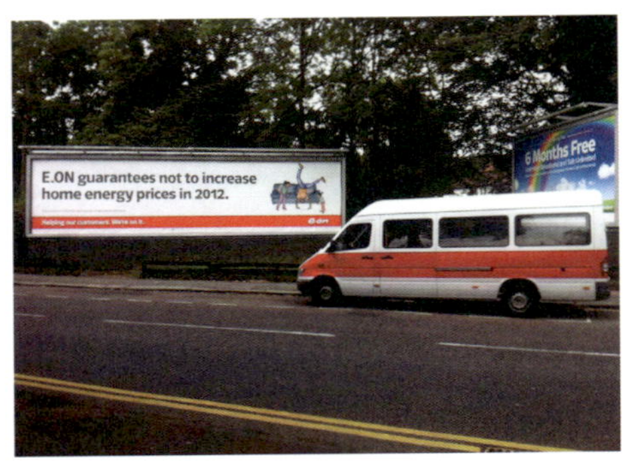

33

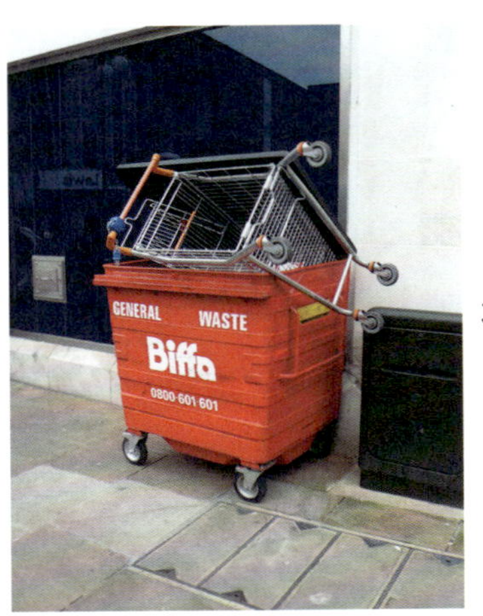

34

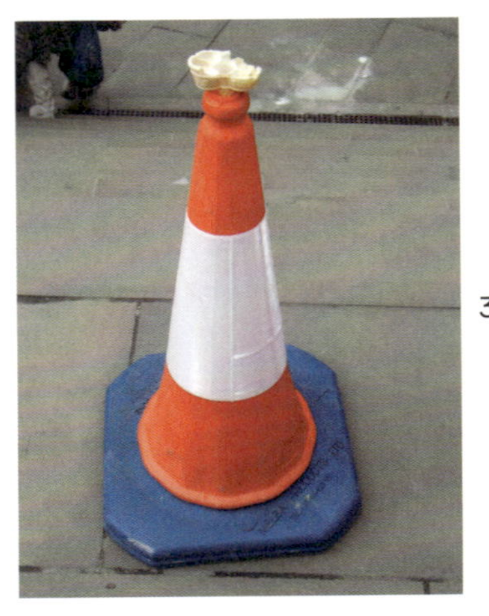

35

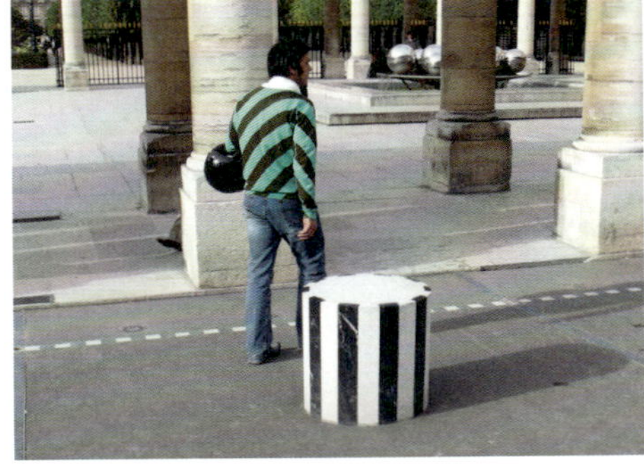

36

all the information that is both implied and withheld in its construction. In terms of the latter, what is withheld, the presentation of sixty-four pairings in this publication also suggests that there may yet be an undocumented Salon des Refusés of objects that in one way or another, refused to coalesce. An undisclosed archive of attempts where $1 \& 1 \neq 1 + 1$.

And yet, given that when combined the objects in question have moved beyond their conventional use value, how is it that they 'succeed'? What aesthetic systems govern not just their creation but their selection here for this publication? In many cases, their innate 'rightness' is often based on a harmony of proportions between otherwise divergent forms, reflecting at a prosaic level the wonder of regularly occurring patterns in nature such as spirals and fractals. In $1+1$ terms, these include the surprising sameness in circumference of an earplug and the gap in a peg; the shared diameter of an ice cream cone and the top of a traffic cone; the equality in diameter of a swimming cap and a watermelon. 'Success' also arises from capturing a certain tension, as well as an acceptance, between things, exemplified here in the cotton wool bud that appears to perfectly bridge the space between headphones, whilst also forcing them apart. Above all, the pairings that work be effortlessly matched rather than forced and that effortlessness must be tangible within the image.

When studying the individual items in question in the manner of an anthropologist hoping to learn more about the social relations that govern their selection it is possible to discern one common factor. Whether organic or man-made, they are all fairly ubiquitous, humble, archetypal everyday things; items we need rather than desire and which more usually sit in the background and middle ground of life. Combined and isolated they have

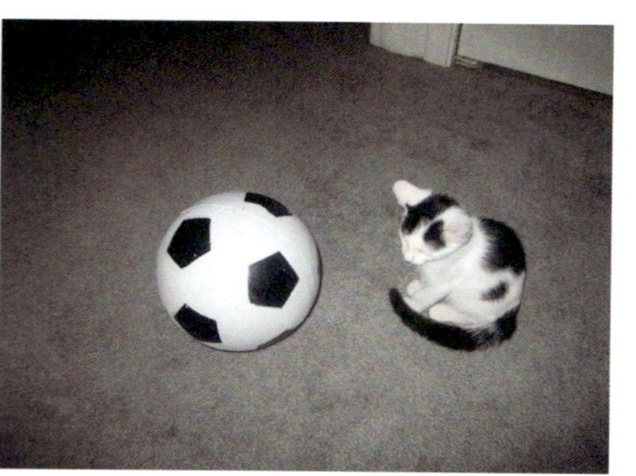

7

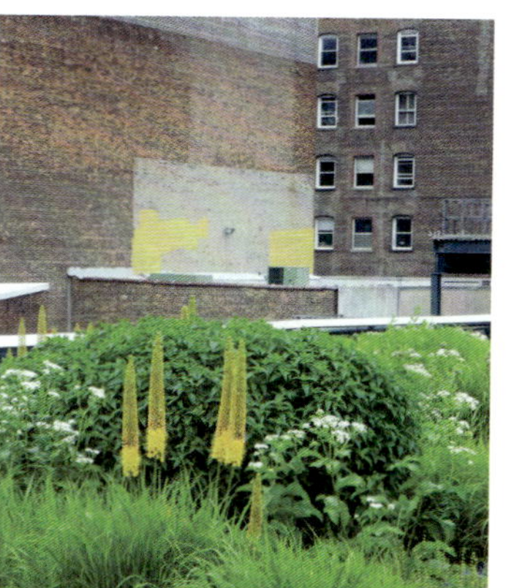

8

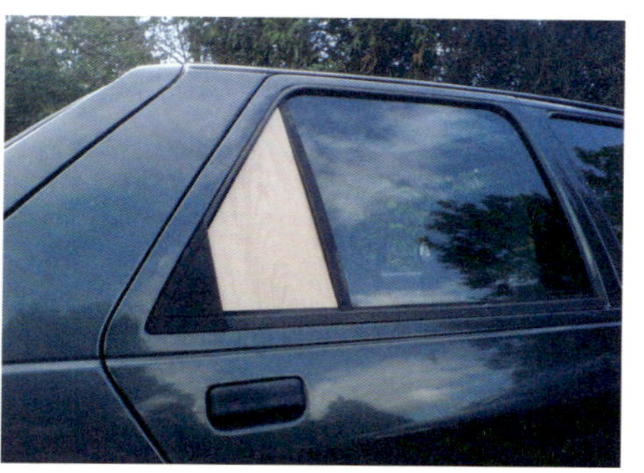

9

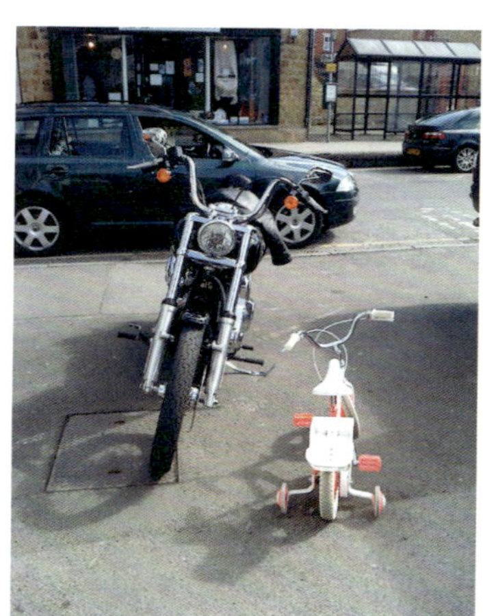

10

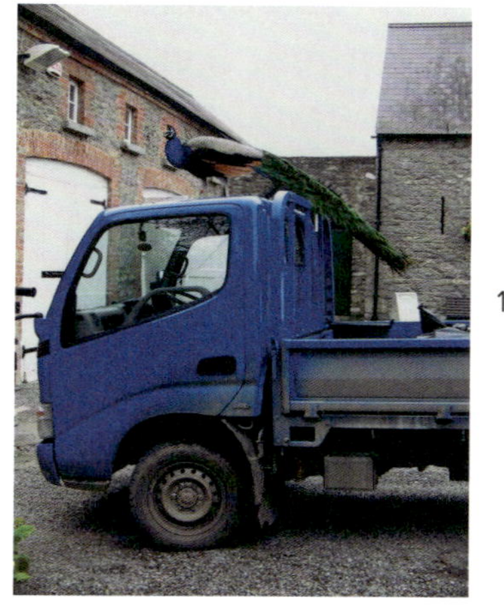

11

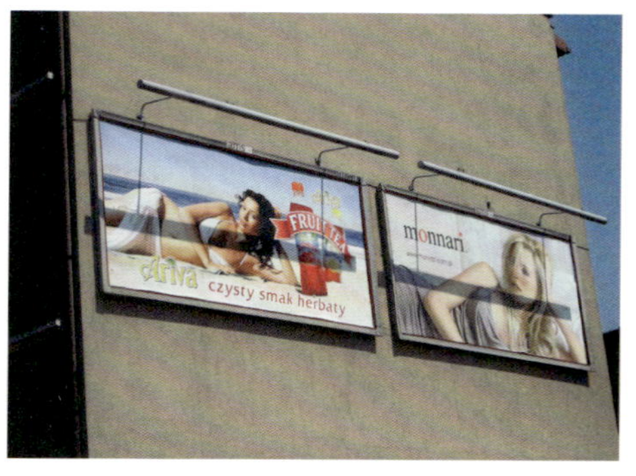

12

been moved to the foreground of our perception and shift in status from generic things to curious hybrid forms which constitute the subject of the work. They are composed of the incidental 'apparatus or equipment'[1] that define us and which Steven Connor identifies as the main concern of his 2011 book <u>Paraphernalia—The Curious Lives of Magical Things</u>. <u>Paraphernalia</u> reflects on the significance of those particular objects which exist at an intimate, graspable level; those which Connor deems the 'fidgetables, things that hold out the possibility of being fiddled with—buttons, elastic bands, pins, sticky tape, glasses'[2] and Connor, like Eatock, is interested in our intimate relationships with objects, in the stories material culture tells about us.

Connor also highlights a particular tactile aspect of our relationship with certain objects through a term J.J. Gibson calls 'affordance'. Connor explains this as 'meaning that they seem to hold out certain very specific kinds of physical invitation to us, often involving an angle of approach or physical address. A teacup asks to be picked up by the handler; a brandy glass invites one to cradle it, tender as a dove, from underneath … a chair irresistibly proposes that one lowers oneself into it backwards. Such objects seem to have us, or certain parts of us imagined in them'.[3] Thus when Connor states that 'we act in accordance with the affordance of objects'[4], it is possible to identify another principle at the heart of Eatock's project; that is to work against the human-centred affordance of objects by letting new possibilities emerge through redetermining objects against and with other objects.

Function therefore surrenders to the poetry of inter-actions between objects. And yet, whilst we are taken out of the frame, Eatock's project is still a humanist one at heart; he is dealing with the things that imply our presence even in our absence, things that may yet

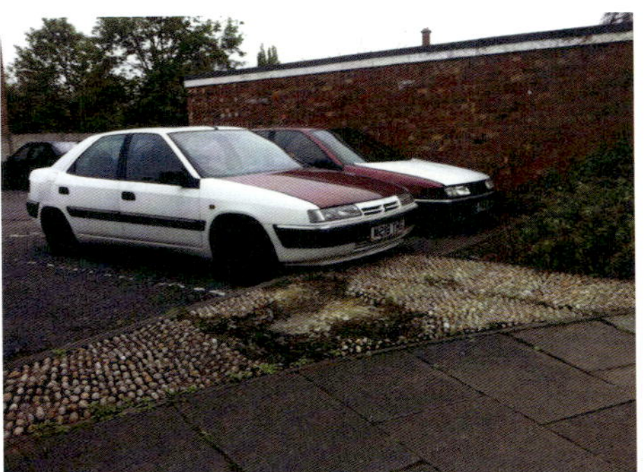

13

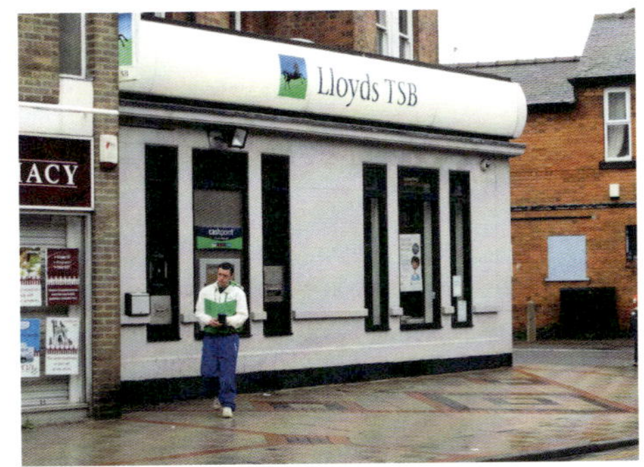

14

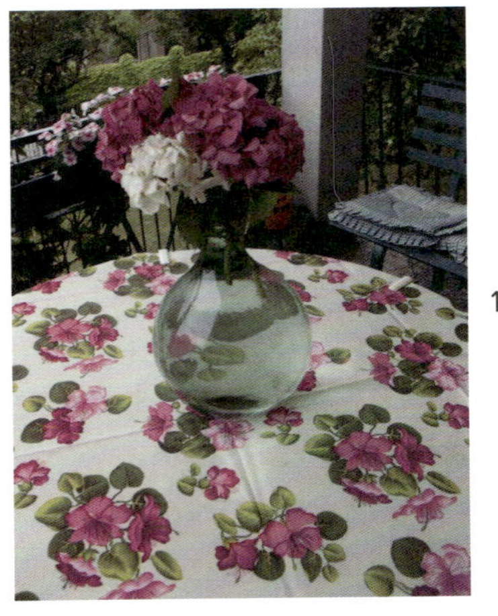

15

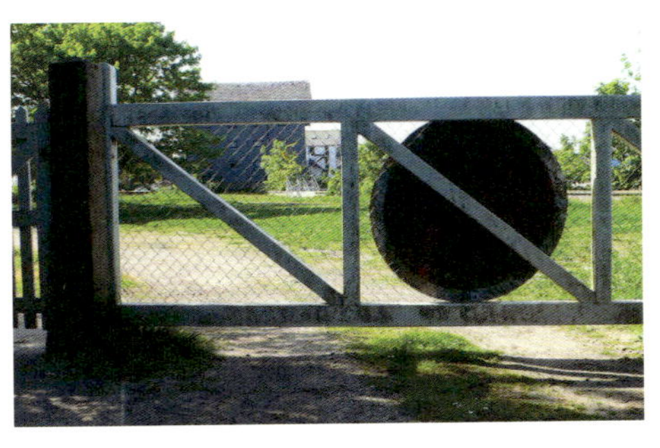

16

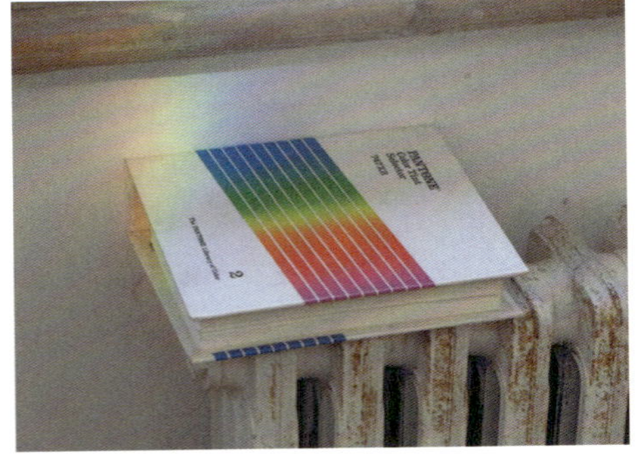

17

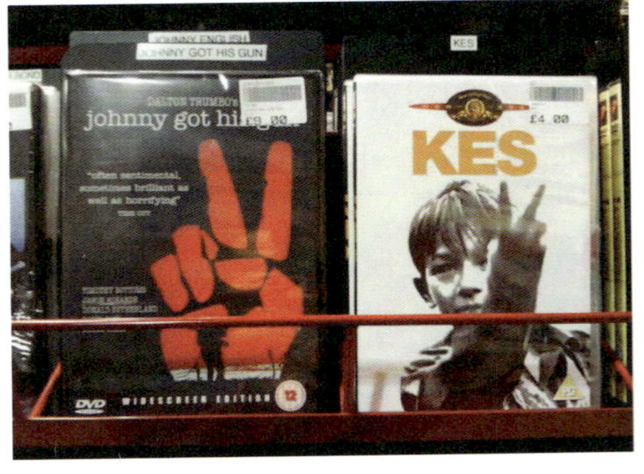

18

scissor jack

shopping basket

shuttlecock

sledgehammer

swimming armbands

swimming cap

teapot

tennis ball

traffic cone

trolley jack

trumpet

umbrella

umbrella clothesline

watering can

watermelon

weights

wheelbarrow

wine glass

yucca

zimmer frame

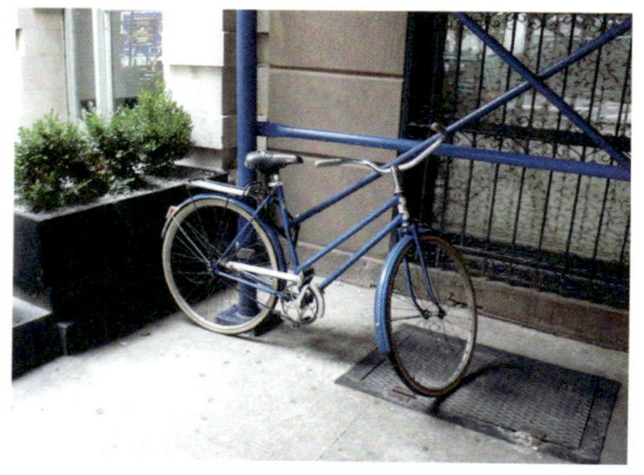

37

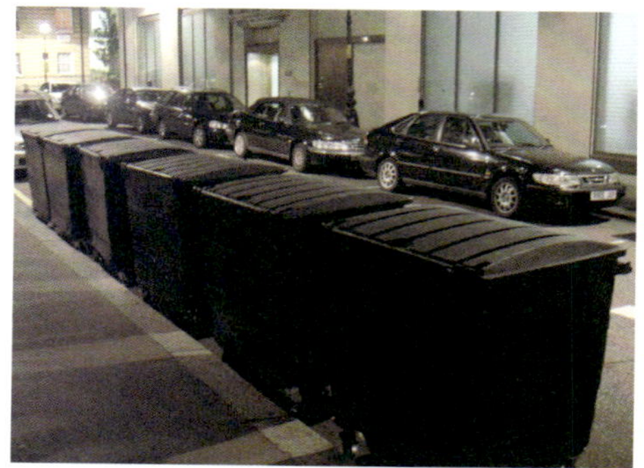

38

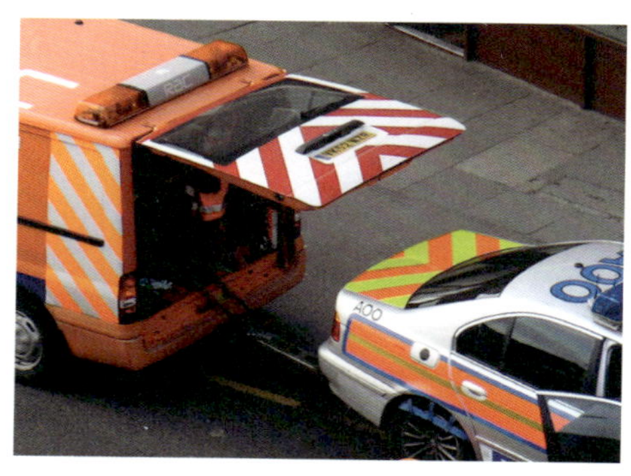

39

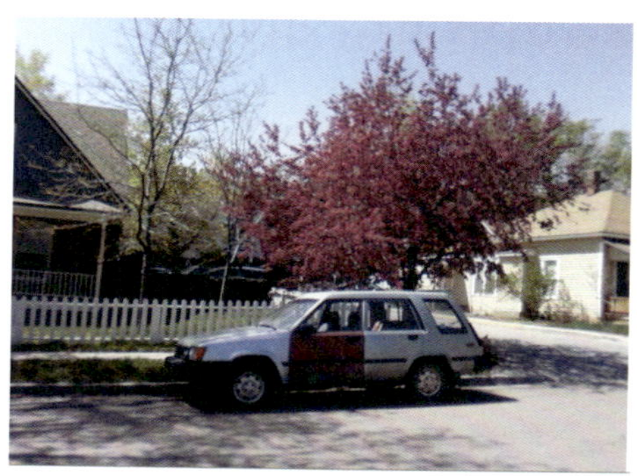

40

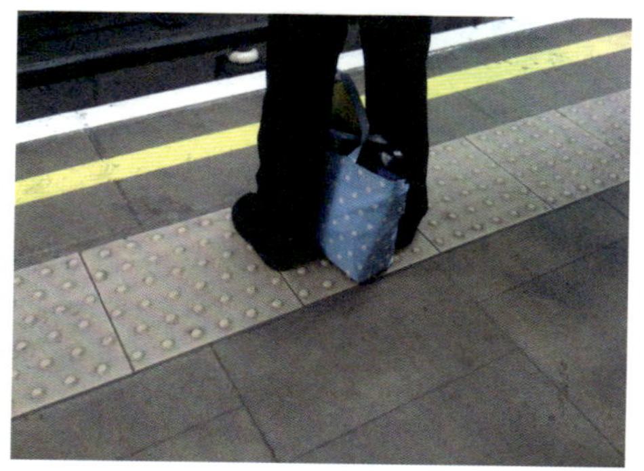

41

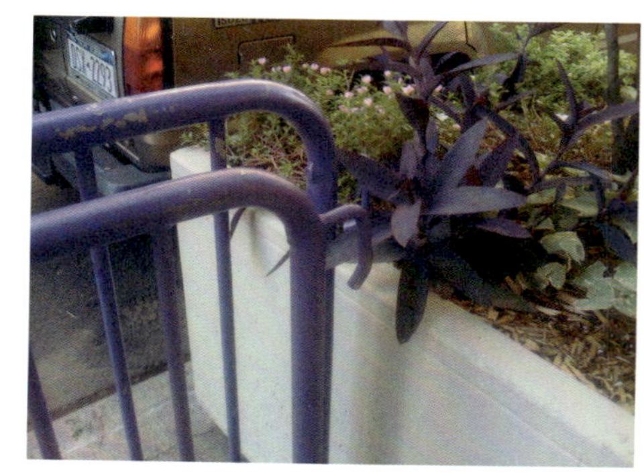

42

flymo

funnel

hammer

headphones

high heeled shoe

ice cream cone

ironing board

ketchup bottle

kickstand

landing net

lifejacket

lipstick

lucky cat

megaphone

nail

oil can

oil drum

parasol base

patio table

plastic cup

pritt stick

radio

rolling dolly

sack trolley

safety helmet

safety tape

Christian Eager   1 25
Maxwell Harrison   2
David Falkner   3
Tim Heiler   4
Nick Hand   5
Alessandra Colombo   6
Brendan Lee   7
Alice Berry   8
Sam Mallett   9
Luke Flynn   10
Judith Stokart   11
Jordan Sheldrick   12
Abre Etteh   13
Gavin Rogers   14
Peter Marigold   15
Simon Jones   16 29 33 38 39 41
David Blamey   17
Nicola Griffiths   18
Alfred Strik Swages   19
Pavlina Morhacova   20
Camille Szklorz   21
Matthew Edgar   22
Lucas van Esch   23
Ollie Langridge   24
Daniel Eatock   26 27 28 34 37
Monica Nannini   30
Martin Brown   31
Tomohide Mizuuchi   32
Alistair Veryard   35
Timothy Evans   36
Rachel Storm   40
Richard Agerbeek   42

Thank You Pictures

To contribute, email your picture and title to
daniel@eatock.com

survive us, as Connor observes, the stuff that will 'constitute something like involuntary abstracts or personal archives, that bear our signatures, have lives in their charge and may one day amount to what we were'.[5] Furthermore, through exploring the myriad potential connections between the paraphernalia of work and leisure, it is also possible to invest emotions in these newly combined forms. Thus amongst the deadpan studies, there is, for example, a distinctive note of poignancy generated by the anthropomorphic zimmer frame which supports heavy weights, as well as more than a hint of slapstick humour from the sledgehammer that balances on an delicate egg in a neat reversal of roles. These emotions and sensations are not integral to the objects themselves in either their individual or combined forms, but are indicative of the productive unstable flow of thoughts and affective projections that go back and forth between the perceiver and the perceived, between the human subject and the object based proposals of 1+1. Therefore, while encapsulating a number of governing principles involving repetition and impermanence, as well as the aesthetic logics of proportion, tension and effortlessness, in order to fully acknowledge the contexts and forces that operate around both image and object, the equation of 1+1 may perhaps be extended to < >1+1< > which in itself, could also stand in for this essay.

Marie-Anne McQuay
is a curator at Spike Island, Bristol

1 p12, Steven Connor, *Paraphernalia—The Curious Lives of Magical Things*, 2011, Profile Books, London.

2 p4, Ibid

3 p2-3, Ibid

4 p4, Ibid

5 p13, Ibid

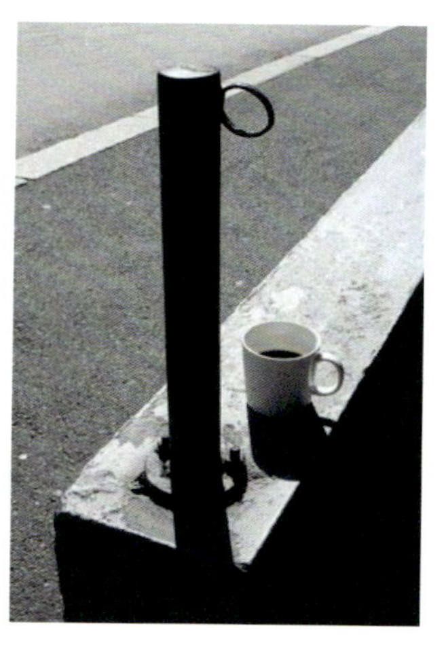

19

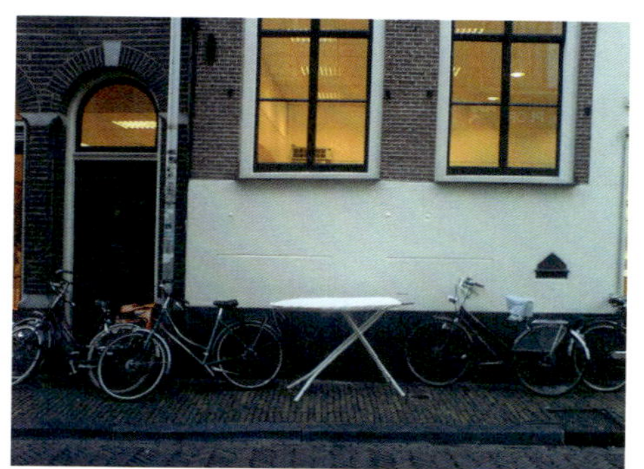

20

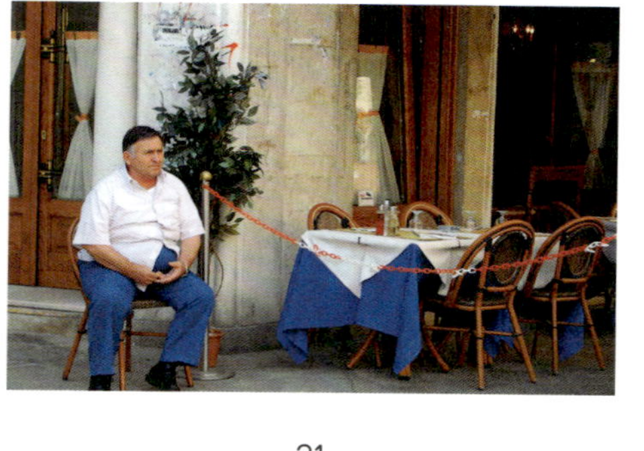

21

22

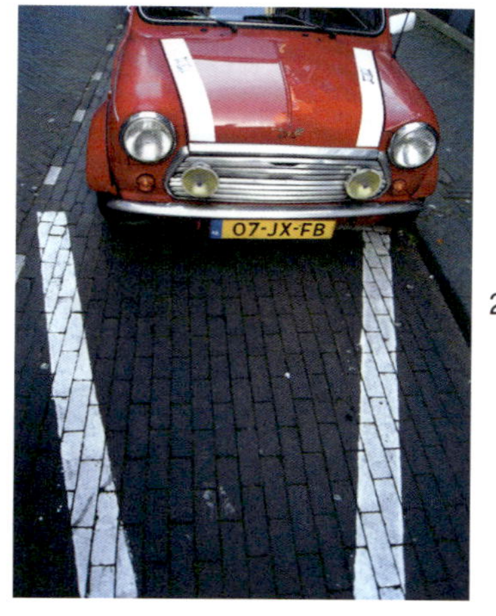

23

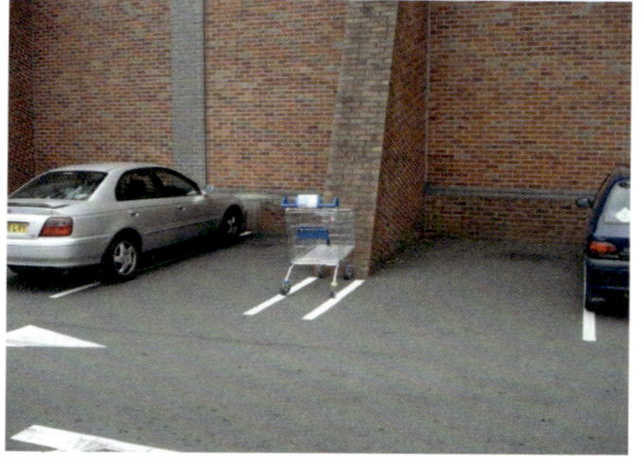

24

< > 1+1 < >
Marie-Anne McQuay

Two key ordering principles based around the properties of repetition and impermanence can be observed in the paired objects arranged by Daniel Eatock during his fellowship at the Stanley Picker Gallery; pairings which appear to follow the simple equation 1+1. Firstly, repetition is only partial: the same item may be used in different configurations, with a basket ball and sink plunger making several notable appearances, however, no two items can be combined together more than once. Secondly, impermanence is integral. Conjoining is only permissible through judicious placement: acts of temporary extension and contraction, inflation and deflation are allowed but no object is irreparably altered. Or, to put it more succinctly, the choice of 1+1 must be unique and always allow for 1+1-1.

At the end of the project, all of the objects used are returned to their original function as they were ultimately once intended. As combinations however, Eatock's index of scenarios ranges from the probable to the surreal; from a yucca plant placed on an artist's stool (something not entirely unlikely to occur in either a studio or domestic situation), to the more unusual and distinctly Freudian spiky phallic cactus perched inside a high heeled shoe. While standardising the manner of their documentation results initially in a visual and temporal leveling, each proposition, on closer inspection, conveys its own particular impression of duration. For example, whereas the oil drum on a drum kit stand transmits a sense of settled solidity that borders on permanence, we are left to speculate whether the nail that lifts the hammer up from the floor lasted only as long as it took to take the photograph. Thus, where once there was a physical presence in real space, now there is only an image with

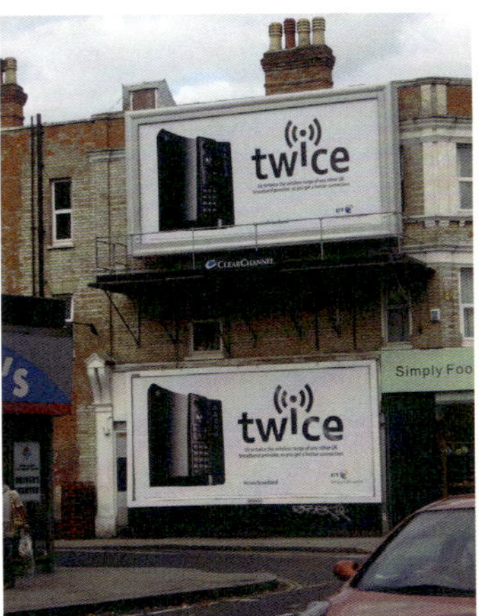

1

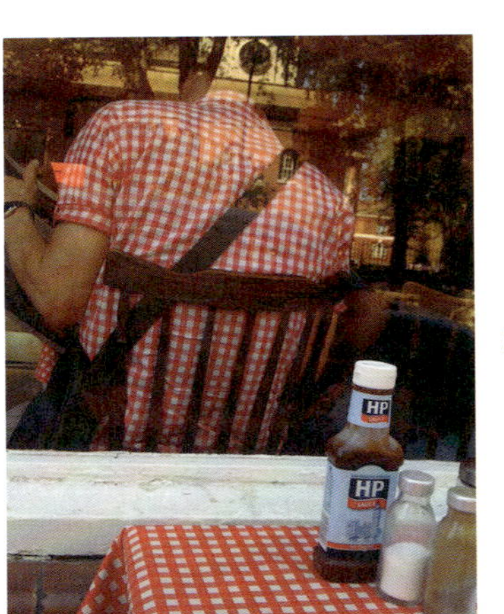

2

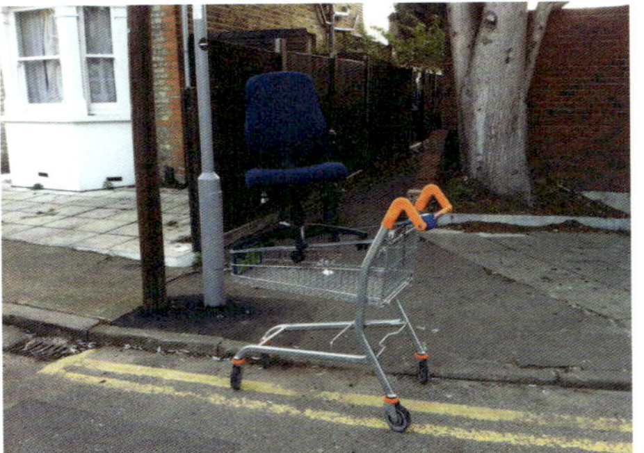

3

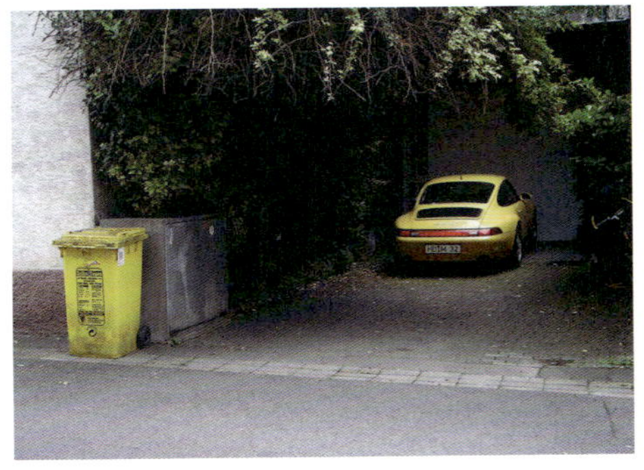

4

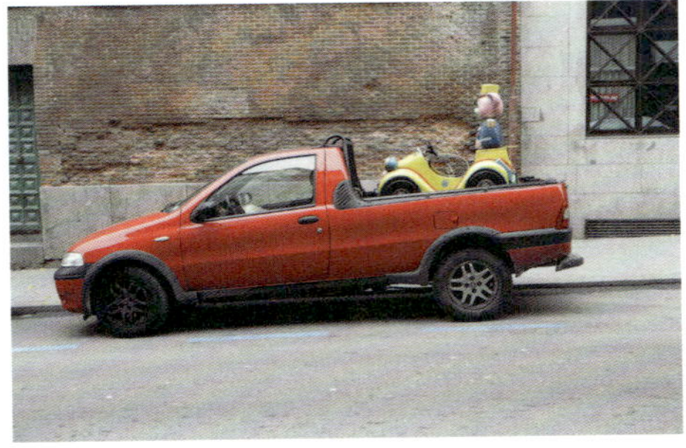

5

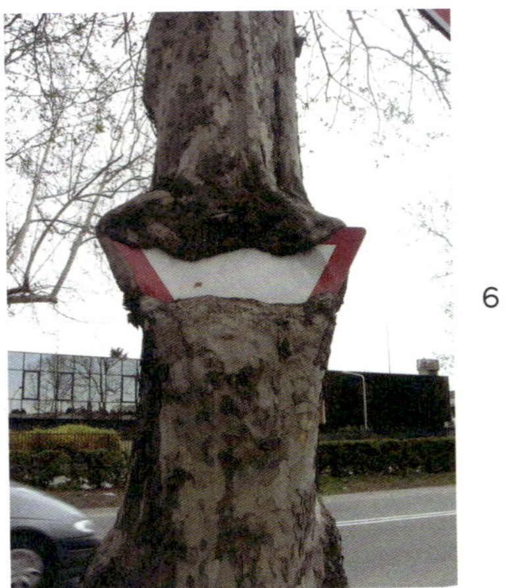

6

o n e   +   1

artist's stool	cotton swab
baby bottle	d lock
balloon	deck chair
banana	desk lamp
basket ball	director's chair
bird cage	diy workbench
bucket	drain plunger
cactus	drop bar
chair	drum stand
clothes drying rack	ear plug
clothes peg	egg
coat hanger	fire extinguisher
cocktail glass	fish bowl

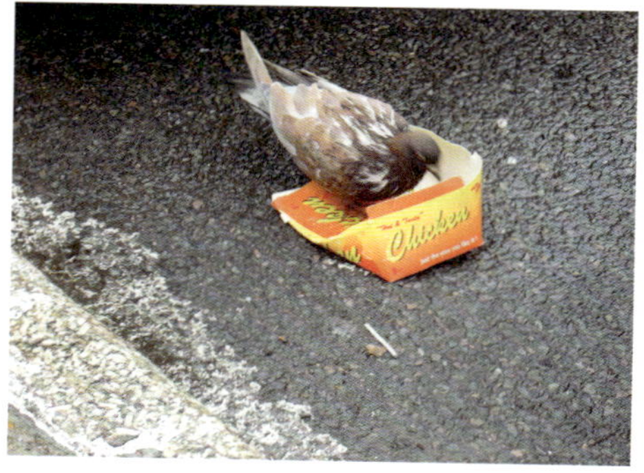

25

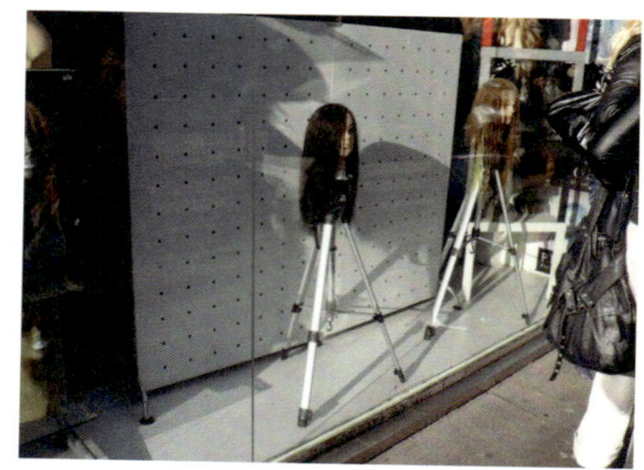

26

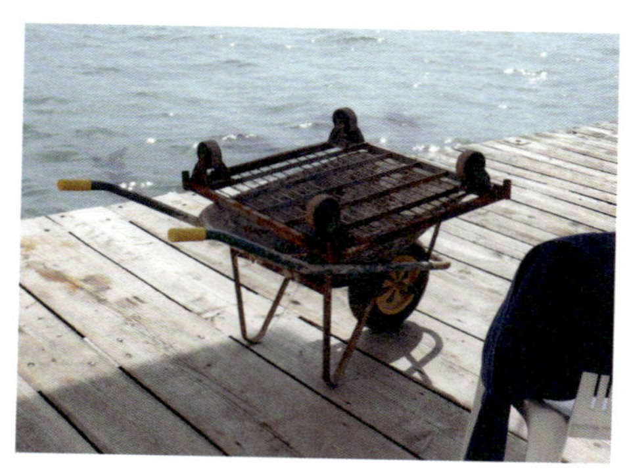

27

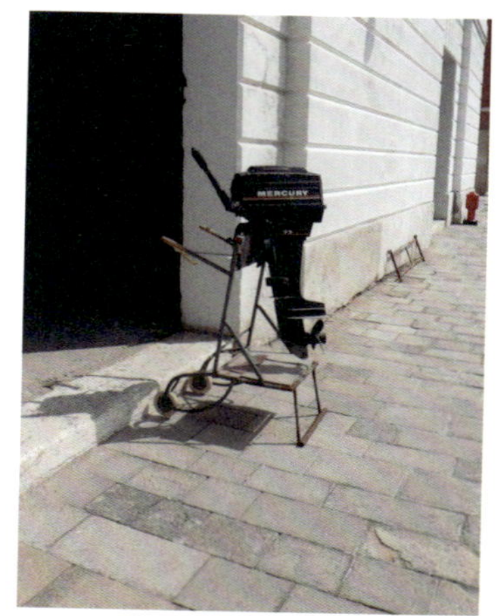

28

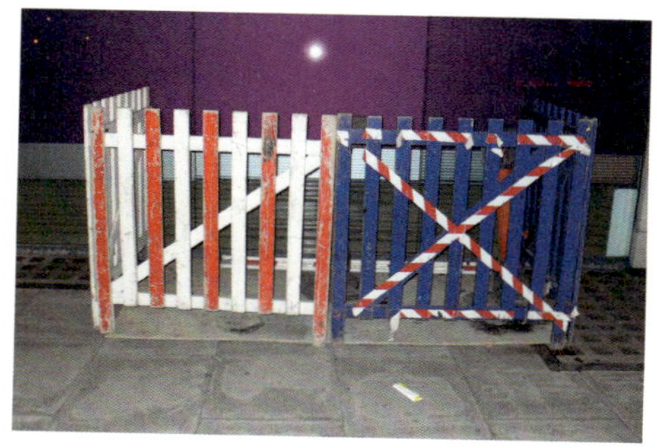

29

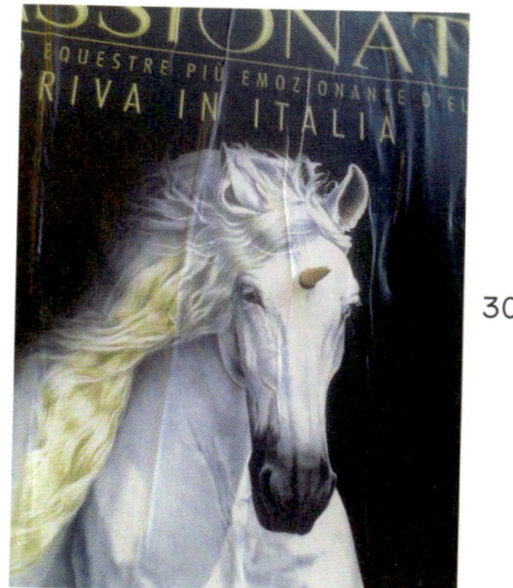

30